LES PETITS PLATS
FRANÇAIS

sensational cupcakes

ALISA MOROV

Photography by Deirdre Rooney
Styling by Élodie Rambaud

MARKS &
SPENCER

Marks and Spencer p.l.c.
PO Box 3339
Chester CH99 9QS

English language edition published in Great Britain by
Simon & Schuster UK Ltd, 2011
A CBS Company

shop online
www.marksandspencer.com

ISBN 8040862
Printed in U.A.E.

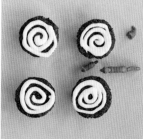

Contents

"Hey Cupcake!"

'Hey, cupcake!' – something an American might say when he or she eats a good cupcake, sees a cupcake or maybe greets a sweetheart!

Your very own little cake. Hold it in your hand, peel the paper away gently and take a bite. The mix of frosting, cake, sometimes a surprise hidden inside... An entire cake, just for you, just your size, the flavour and colour of your choosing. Made well, with good ingredients, care and imagination. Delicious.

After living outside the USA for a few years, I learned that the American cupcake is not the same as cupcakes or fairy cakes from other countries and cultures. The American cupcake has its very own texture, taste and form.

These are quintessential American cupcake recipes. You will find the basics (vanilla or chocolate) dense or airy, and you will find inspired variations. And no matter what, they remain American in texture and taste.

Equipment

electric mixer
paper cases
cupcake moulds
cooling rack
spatulas, spoons, whisks
measuring cups and spoons
sieve
timer

Hints and tips

It is very important to follow the recipe as written, use the ingredients noted and adhere to the right oven temperatures. Having an independent thermometer in your oven will help. An oven that is too hot or too cool will result in cupcakes that fall in the centre or overflow out of the mould. For most of the recipes, unless noted otherwise, the little cakes are fully baked when a skewer inserted into the middle of the cupcake comes out clean. As with any type of cooking, use the highest quality ingredients available.

Before starting a recipe, prepare the cupcake trays with paper cases and preheat the oven. Cupcake moulds and cases come in a variety of shapes and sizes. Most recipes can be made large, medium or small size.

Allow the cupcakes to cool to room temperature before applying any toppings. Once decorated, they can be kept refrigerated for 3 days. Undecorated cupcakes can be refrigerated for up to 5 days, or frozen for up to 2 months. Thaw completely before applying any toppings.

Cupcake bases

Light vanilla cupcakes
This cupcake is lighter than the basic cupcake.

Preparation time: 20 minutes
Cooking time: 25–30 minutes
Makes 24 large cupcakes

60 ml (2 fl oz) whole milk
4 large egg whites
1 teaspoon vanilla extract
225 g (8 oz) plain flour
200 g (7 oz) caster sugar
1 teaspoon baking powder
½ teaspoon salt
1 teaspoon ground cardamom
190 g (6¾ oz) unsalted butter

Preheat the oven to 170°C (fan oven 150°C), Gas Mark 3½.

Mix the milk, egg whites and vanilla extract together in a medium sized bowl and set aside. Place the dry ingredients in a large bowl and mix slowly for a few seconds to blend well. Add the butter to the dry ingredients and half of the egg mixture. Mix slowly until everything looks moist. Beat vigorously for 1 minute.

Add the remaining egg mixture in two batches, beating for 30 seconds each time. Beat again for 10 seconds. Spoon the batter into cupcake moulds lined with paper cases. Fill the cases three-quarters full, as these do not rise as much as others. Bake for 25–30 minutes until a skewer inserted into a cake comes out clean.

Pound cake cupcakes
This cupcake is denser and heavier than the basic cupcake and holds up to additions of fruit very well.

Preparation time: 20 minutes
Cooking time: 25–30 minutes
Makes 12 large cupcakes.

45 ml (1½ fl oz) whole milk
3 large eggs
1 teaspoon vanilla extract
170 g (6 oz) plain flour
150 g (5¼ oz) caster sugar
¾ teaspoon baking powder
¼ teaspoon salt
150 g (5¼ oz) unsalted butter

Preheat the oven to 170°C (fan oven 150°C), Gas Mark 3½.

Mix the milk, eggs and vanilla extract together and set aside. Place the dry ingredients in large mixing bowl and mix slowly for a few seconds to blend well. Add the butter to the dry ingredients and half of the egg mixture. Mix slowly until everything looks moist. Beat vigorously for 1 minute.

Add the remaining egg mixture and beat well for 1 minute. Spoon the batter into cupcake moulds lined with paper cases. Fill half to two-thirds full, depending on how high a dome you want on the finished cupcake. Bake for 25–30 minutes until a skewer inserted into a cake comes out clean.

Buttercreams and other toppings

The definition of buttercream differs from country to country. These are ones I grew up with in the USA. Try mixing and matching with different cupcakes and let your imagination go. Once you have decorated your cupcakes, you may need to put them in the fridge to harden the topping. Decorate before the topping is set.

Italian meringue

Makes 475 g (1 lb 1 oz)

4 large egg whites
200 g (7 oz) icing sugar
1 teaspoon vanilla extract

Place the egg whites and icing sugar in a metal bowl and place over a pan of simmering water. Whisk until the sugar has completely dissolved. Remove from the heat and beat on a low speed for 1 minute then slowly increase to high. Continue to beat until the meringue forms shiny, stiff peaks. Mix in the vanilla extract. Use immediately – it will begin to harden. After 8–10 minutes you can brown the meringue with a cook's blowtorch.

Cream cheese frosting

Makes 800 g (1 lb 12 oz)

340 g (12 oz) cream cheese, at room temperature
340 g (12 oz) unsalted butter, at room temperature
1½ teaspoons vanilla extract
450 g (16 oz) icing sugar

Beat the cream cheese, butter and vanilla extract together until smooth. Add the icing sugar slowly and beat until light and fluffy. Refrigerate for 30–40 minutes before using. This can be kept in the refrigerator for up to 6 days.

Vanilla buttercream

Makes 500–600 g (1 lb 5 oz)

200 g (7 oz) unsalted butter
800 g (1 lb 12 oz) icing sugar
120 ml (4¼ fl oz) double cream
2 teaspoons vanilla extract

Using a mixer, mix the butter and half the sugar for 30 seconds, then add the cream and vanilla extract. Mix until creamy. Gradually add the rest of the sugar, one cup at a time, beating well after each addition. Continue to beat until the frosting is thick. Use immediately or store in an airtight container at room temperature for up to 3 days.

Chocolate buttercream

Makes 400–500 g (1 lb 1 oz)

155 g (5½ oz) dark chocolate (70% cocoa solids)
340 g (12 oz) unsalted butter
2 tablespoons double cream

Melt the chocolate in a bowl over a pan of simmering water. Remove from the heat and allow to cool for about 10 minutes. Beat the butter until creamy. Slowly add the cream and continue to beat until smooth. Gradually add the chocolate and continue to beat until creamy. Use immediately or store in an airtight container at room temperature for 2 days.

Vanilla-vanilla

'When you look at a cupcake, you've got to smile.' Anne Byrn.
This is THE cupcake! It is dense and delicious, with a taste that improves after 1 or 2 days.

Preparation time: 20 minutes + cooling
Cooking time: 30–35 minutes
Makes 24 large cupcakes

Vanilla cupcakes
435 g (15¼ oz) plain flour
1 tablespoon baking powder
1 teaspoon bicarbonate of soda
½ teaspoon salt
190 g (6¾ oz) unsalted butter
400 g (14 oz) caster sugar
4 large eggs
300 ml (10½ fl oz) buttermilk
1½ teaspoons vanilla extract

Vanilla buttercream
(see recipe on page 10)

Preheat the oven to 170°C (fan oven 150°C), Gas Mark 3½.

Sift the flour, baking powder, bicarbonate of soda and salt together, and set aside.

In a bowl and using an electric mixer, beat the butter until soft. Slowly add the sugar and beat for about 3 minutes until light and fluffy. Add the eggs, one at a time, beating for 20 seconds after each addition and scraping down the sides of the bowl.

In a small bowl, mix the buttermilk with the vanilla extract. In three stages, slowly add the sifted dry ingredients to the creamed butter and sugar, alternating with the buttermilk mixture. Begin and end with the flour mixture. Be careful not to overmix.

Spoon the batter into cupcake moulds lined with paper cases until they are two-thirds full.

Bake for 30–35 minutes until a skewer inserted into a cake comes out clean. Leave to cool completely.

Make the vanilla buttercream following the method on page 10 and pipe on with a wide, 5-point star nozzle.

Tip: These are best if made a day ahead of applying the buttercream. Store (decorated or plain) in an airtight container for up to 2 days or in the refrigerator for a week. Freeze undecorated for up to 2 months.

Chocolate-chocolate

Okay, so perhaps this is THE cupcake. It is just as delicious as the Vanilla-vanilla (see page 12) but it's chocolate! Rich, deep, melt in your mouth chocolate.

Preparation time: 20 minutes + cooling
Cooking time: 20–25 minutes
Makes 24 large cupcakes

Chocolate cupcakes
75 g (2½ oz) cocoa powder
300 ml (10½ fl oz) boiling water
3 large eggs
1 teaspoon vanilla extract
1 teaspoon chocolate extract (optional)
280 g (10 oz) plain flour
300 g (10½ oz) caster sugar
1 tablespoon baking powder
¾ teaspoon salt
190 g (6¾ oz) unsalted butter

Chocolate buttercream
(see recipe on page 10)

Preheat the oven to 160°C (fan oven 140°C), Gas Mark 3.

Mix the cocoa powder and boiling water together in a small bowl until smooth. Set aside.

Mix the eggs, a quarter of the cocoa mixture and the vanilla and chocolate extracts together in a medium bowl

In a large mixing bowl, combine the remaining dry ingredients and slowly mix with a whisk. Using an electric mixer, add the butter and remaining cocoa mixture and beat slowly until all the dry ingredients are moist. Increase the speed to medium and beat for 1–2 minutes. Scrape down the sides then add the egg mixture in two batches, beating for 30 seconds after each addition and scraping down the sides.

Spoon the batter into cupcake moulds lined with paper cases until they are three-quarters full.

Bake for 20–25 minutes until a skewer inserted into a cake comes out clean. The cupcakes will rise while baking and fall back a bit while cooling. Leave to cool completely.

Make the chocolate buttercream following the method on page 10 and pipe on with a narrow, 6-point star nozzle.

Store (decorated or plain) in an airtight container for up to 2 days or in the refrigerator for a week. Freeze undecorated for up to 2 months.

Carrot cupcakes with cream cheese frosting

In the mid 1970s, this recipe was given to me on a small piece of paper - it remains one of my most cherished possessions.

Preparation time: 20 minutes + cooling
Cooking time: 25–35 minutes
Makes 12–16 large cupcakes

Carrot cupcakes
190 g (6¾ oz) plain flour
275 g (9¾ oz) caster sugar
½ teaspoon salt
1½ teaspoons baking soda
¾ teaspoon ground cinnamon
175 ml (6¼ fl oz) vegetable oil
2 large eggs
1½ teaspoons vanilla extract
90 g (3 oz) chopped walnuts
120 g (4¼ oz) grated carrots
75 g (2½ oz) tinned pineapple, chopped

Cream cheese frosting
(see recipe on page 10)

Preheat the oven to 150°C (fan oven 130°C), Gas Mark 2.

Sift all the dry ingredients into a bowl. Add the oil, eggs and vanilla extract and beat well. Mix in the walnuts, carrots and pineapple.

Half-fill cupcake moulds lined with paper cases with the batter. Bake for 25–35 minutes until a skewer inserted into a cake comes out clean. Leave to cool completely.

Make the cream cheese frosting following the method on page 10 and decorate the cupcakes.

Store iced or plain in an airtight container for up to 2 days or in the refrigerator for a week, or freeze for up to 1 month.

Vanilla cupcakes with salted butter caramel frosting

Sweet and salty....a wonderful combination.

Preparation time: 25 minutes + cooling
Cooking time: 30–35 minutes
Makes 24 large cupcakes

Vanilla cupcakes
(see recipe on page 12)

Salted butter caramel frosting
200 g (7 oz) salted butter, at room temperature
300 g (10½ oz) icing sugar
165 g (5¾ oz) brown sugar
60 ml (2 fl oz) milk
1 dessertspoon corn syrup
1 teaspoon vanilla extract

Make the vanilla cupcakes following the method on page 12. Leave to cool completely.

Using an electric mixer, cream the butter then add the sugars, beating slowly for about 2 minutes. Add the milk, corn syrup and vanilla extract and continue to beat until smooth and creamy, about 4 minutes.

Store in an airtight container at room temperature for up to 3 days. The frosting will set if placed in the refrigerator.

Decorate the cupcakes as you wish.

Dark chocolate cupcakes with fennel buttercream

In Brussels, there's a chocolate shop that mixes herb seeds into their chocolate. This gave me the idea to turn this into a cupcake. It has become a favourite for everyone who has taken a bite.

Preparation time: 30 minutes
Cooking time: 20–25 minutes
Makes 24 large cupcakes

Chocolate cupcakes
(see recipe on page 14)

Fennel buttercream
2 dessertspoons dried
  fennel seeds
200 g (7 oz) unsalted butter,
  at room temperature
800 g (1 lb 11 oz) icing sugar
120 ml (4¼ fl oz) double cream

golden dragées, to decorate

Make the chocolate cupcakes following the method on page 14. Fill the paper cases three-quarters full to get a higher cupcake top. Leave to cool completely.

Gently grind the fennel seeds in a pestle and mortar or an electric grinder, leaving some of the seeds whole. You don't want a powder.

Put the butter and half the sugar in a large mixing bowl. Using an electic mixer, mix for 30 seconds then add the cream and the ground fennel. Mix on a medium speed until smooth and creamy, about 4 minutes.

Gradually add the rest of the sugar, bit by bit, beating very well after each addition, about 1 minute. Continue to beat until the buttercream has reached a thickness to spread well. Use immediately or store in an airtight container at room temperature for up to 3 days. The frosting will set when placed in the refrigerator.

Frost the cupcakes with the fennel buttercream and decorate with golden dragées.

Pear cupcakes with vanilla buttercream

Et voila! An elegant little cupcake. Lovely to look at, with a variety of textures and flavours that will make you say, 'wow'!

Preparation time: 40 minutes + cooling
Cooking time: 40–50 minutes + 1–2 hours for the pear slices
Makes 12 large cupcakes

Pear cupcakes
2 medium pears, not too ripe, cored and cut into 2 cm (¾ inch cubes)
220 g (7¾ oz) plain flour
1½ teaspoons cinnamon
½ teaspoon baking powder
145 g (5 oz) unsalted butter, at room temperature
300 g (10½ oz) caster sugar
3 eggs

Oven-dried pear slices
1 medium pear, not too ripe
juice of ½ lemon
200 g (7 oz) caster sugar
235 ml (8¼ fl oz) water

Vanilla buttercream
(see recipe on page 10)

Preheat the oven to 170°C (fan oven 150°C), Gas Mark 3½. Line cupcake moulds with paper cases and place 2–3 cubes of pear in the centre of each case, reserving the rest for later.

Mix the flour, cinnamon and baking powder together. Set aside.

In a bowl, beat the butter and sugar together until light and fluffy. Add the eggs and beat well for about 1 minute. Add the dry ingredients and mix slowly until combined. Do not overmix.

Spoon 1½ tablespoons of batter into each mould, on top of the pear cubes. Share the remaining pear cubes evenly between the moulds and gently push them into the batter. Bake for 40–50 minutes until a skewer inserted into a cake comes out clean. Let the cakes cool completely before decorating.

To make the pear slices, line a baking sheet with baking parchment. Slice the pears as thinly as possible, retaining the seeds and stem. Squeeze the lemon juice over them.

Place the sugar and water in a pan and bring to the boil, stirring occasionally, until the sugar has dissolved. Reduce the heat to low and add the pear slices. Cook for 2–3 minutes.

Gently remove the pears and place them on the baking sheet. Bake for 1–2 hours at 90°C (fan oven 70°C), Gas Mark ¼, until they feel dry. Gently turn them over and bake for 10–15 more minutes. Set aside to cool completely.

Make the vanilla buttercream following the method on page 10, decorate the cupcakes and top with a pear slice.

Banana cupcakes with dark chocolate ganache

Preparation time: 20 minutes + cooling
Cooking time: 20–25 minutes
Makes 12–16 cupcakes

Banana cupcakes
2 medium ripe bananas, mashed
30 g (1 oz) crème fraîche
2 large eggs
2 teaspoons lemon zest
1 teaspoon vanilla extract
240 g (8½ oz) plain flour
170 g (6 oz) caster sugar
1 teaspoon baking soda
1 teaspoon baking powder
½ teaspoon salt
130 g (4½ oz) unsalted butter

Dark chocolate ganache
385 ml (13 fl oz) double cream
340 g (12 oz) dark chocolate, broken into small pieces
40 g (1½ oz) unsalted butter, at room temperature

Preheat the oven to 170°C (fan oven 150°C), Gas Mark 3½.

Mix the bananas and crème fraîche together until very smooth. Add the eggs, lemon zest and vanilla extract and mix well.

Sift the flour into a large mixing bowl, add all the other dry ingredients and whisk using an electic mixer. Add the butter and the banana mixture, mix slowly until well combined, then increase the speed and beat for 1 minute. Scrape down the sides.

Use the batter to two-thirds fill cupcake moulds lined with paper cases. Bake for 20–25 minutes until a skewer inserted into a cake comes out clean. Leave to cool before decorating.

To make the ganache, warm the cream until it almost boils then remove from the heat. Add the chocolate to the cream and stir slowly and continuously until smooth. Add the butter and mix well. Leave to cool for about 10 minutes before using.

Ice each cupcake with about 2 teaspoons of ganache. Pour over the centre so that it runs slowly over the sides. Leave the ganache to cool completely until firm and shiny.

Store in an airtight container for up to 2 days.

Brownie cupcakes with peanut butter buttercream

There is a well known rumour that Elvis really liked peanut butter. And while I was growing up, the combination of peanut butter and chocolate came to be known as 'two great tastes, that taste great together'. Which, then, of course… led to this cupcake.

Preparation time: 25 minutes + cooling
Cooking time: 20–25 minutes
Makes 24 large cupcakes

Brownie cupcakes
70 g (2½ oz) cocoa powder
230 ml (8 fl oz) boiling water
3 large eggs
1 teaspoon vanilla extract
1 teaspoon chocolate extract (optional)
140 g (5 oz) peanuts, salted or unsalted
280 g (10 oz) plain flour
300 g (10½ oz) caster sugar
1 tablespoon baking powder
¾ teaspoon salt
190 g (6¾ oz) unsalted butter

Peanut butter buttercream
250 g (8¾ oz) crunchy peanut butter, at room temperature
200 g (7 oz) salted butter, at room temperature
225 g (8 oz) icing sugar

golden dragées to decorate

Preheat the oven to 160°C (fan oven 140°C), Gas Mark 3.

Mix the cocoa powder and boiling water together in small bowl, until the cocoa powder has dissolved completely.

Mix the eggs, a quarter of the cocoa mixture and the vanilla and chocolate extracts together.

In a large mixing bowl combine the peanuts and the remaining dry ingredients and whisk slowly using an electric mixer. Add the butter and the remaining cocoa mixture and beat slowly, until all the dry ingredients are moist. Increase the speed to medium and beat for 1–2 minutes. Scrape down the sides, then add the egg mixture in two batches, beating for 30 seconds after each addition and scraping down the sides.

Line the cupcake moulds with paper cases and fill to halfway. Bake for 20–25 minutes until a skewer inserted into a cake comes out clean. The cupcakes will rise while baking and fall back a bit while cooling. Leave to cool completely.

Using an electric mixer with a paddle attachment, mix the peanut butter and butter together slowly until well combined. Gradually add the sugar and mix well. The icing can be used immediately or stored at room temperature for 3 days.

Decorate the cakes using a piping bag without a nozzle. Cut the piping bag, making a 2 cm (¾ inch) hole, then pipe on. Decorate with gold dragées.

Reproduction of 'Hello Baby' by Melissa Markell, with the kind permission of the artist.

Angel cupcakes

As light as an angel… Okay, a cupcake that fits into a diet is a silly thing to try to obtain. BUT, this is a bit lower in calories than the others, much lighter in texture and just as satisfying!

Preparation time: 25 minutes + cooling
Cooking time: 25–30 minutes
Makes 24 large cupcakes

pink sugar sprinkles (optional), to decorate

Light vanilla cupcakes
(see recipe on page 8)

Vanilla buttercream
200 g (7 oz) unsalted butter, at room temperature
800 g (1 lb 11 oz) icing sugar
120 ml (4¼ fl oz) double cream
2 teaspoons vanilla extract
liquid or powdered pink food colouring

Make the cupcakes following the light vanilla cupcakes method on page 8. Leave to cool completely.

For the buttercream, put the butter and half the sugar in a large mixing bowl and mix for 30 seconds using an electric mixer. Add the cream and vanilla extract. Mix on a medium speed for around 4 minutes, until smooth and creamy.

Gradually add the rest of the sugar, mixing well between each addition.

Add the food colouring little by little until you have the colour you want. Continue to beat until the icing is thick and spreadable (you can test this on the back of a wooden spoon).

Decorate with the buttercream using a large, 5-point star nozzle. Finish with a pinch of pink sugar sprinkles, if you wish.

Use immediately or store in an airtight container at room temperature for up to 3 days. The frosting will set when placed in the refrigerator.

Raspberry ricotta cupcakes

Raspberries, ricotta and pine nuts – these only need a dusting of icing sugar. But if you choose to add one of the basic frostings to this already yummy morsel, well… 'That would be the icing on the cake!'

Preparation time: 20 minutes +
30 minutes draining + cooling
Cooking time: 30–40 minutes
Makes 12 large cupcakes

Raspberry cupcakes
375 g (13¼ oz) raspberries, frozen
  or fresh
250 g (8¾ oz) ricotta cheese
3 medium eggs
1 egg yolk
250 g (8¾ oz) caster sugar
finely grated zest of 1 lemon
225 g (8 oz) self-raising flour
60 ml (2 fl oz) cognac or brandy
¼ teaspoon cinnamon
3 tablespoons pine nuts, toasted

Preheat the oven to 190°C (fan oven 170°C), Gas Mark 5.

Line cupcake moulds with paper cases and place two or three raspberries in each case, reserving the rest for later. Frozen berries actually work better than fresh. If you are using fresh, remember that they are a bit fragile.

Drain the ricotta in a mesh sieve for 30 minutes. Beat with a whisk until smooth then set aside.

Using an electric mixer with a paddle attachment, beat the eggs, egg yolk and sugar until pale in colour and thick. Add the lemon zest and beat for 20 seconds. Add the ricotta and mix on a medium speed until well combined.

Slowly add the flour in three batches, scraping down the sides after each addition. Finally, mix in the cognac or brandy, cinnamon and pine nuts. Be careful not to overwork the mixture.

Divide the batter between the paper cases, spooning it over the raspberries until the cases are about half full. Gently push two or three more raspberries into each cake. Bake for 30–40 minutes until a skewer inserted into a cake comes out clean.

Store in an airtight container for up to 3 days or in the refrigerator for up to a week.

Earl Grey cupcakes

Make these in different sizes – the batter is so versatile that it works even in the smallest size. This is based on the pound cake cupcake recipe, with a few alterations.

Preparation time: 20 minutes + cooling
Cooking time: 25–30 minutes
Makes 12 large cupcakes

Earl Grey cupcakes
45 ml (1½ oz) whole milk
2 tablespoons dry Earl Grey tea leaves
3 large eggs
½ teaspoon vanilla extract
170 g (6 oz) plain flour
150 g (5¼ oz) caster sugar
¾ teaspoon baking powder
¼ teaspoon salt
150 g (5¼ oz) unsalted butter

Vanilla buttercream
(see recipe on page 10)
liquid or powdered dark pink food colouring
silver dragées to decorate

Preheat the oven to 170°C (fan oven 150°C), Gas Mark 3½.

Warm the milk and use it to steep 1 tablespoon of tea for 4 minutes. Remove from the heat, strain to discard the tea and set the milk aside. Grind the remaining tea leaves to a fine powder with a pestle and mortar or an electric grinder and set aside.

Mix the milk, eggs and vanilla extract in a medium sized bowl.

Place all the dry ingredients, including the ground tea, in a large mixing bowl. Using an electric mixer, mix slowly for a few seconds to blend well. Add the butter and half of the egg mixture. Mix slowly until everything looks moist. Increase the speed and beat for 1 minute.

Scrape down the sides, add the remaining egg mixture and beat well for 1 minute. Spoon the batter into cupcake moulds lined with paper cases. Fill half to two-thirds full, depending on how high a dome you want on the finished cupcake.

Bake for 25–30 minutes until a skewer inserted into a cake comes out clean. Leave to cool completely.

Make the vanilla buttercream following the method on page 10. Add a little dark pink food colouring to the buttercream and decorate the cupcakes.

Red velvet cupcakes

Red velvet cake is a traditional Southern American recipe. Finding the definitive, original recipe proved elusive. I tasted many samples – some great, some not so good. But I knew what my goal was. After months of experimentation, I arrived at a red velvet cupcake that is as good as the great ones of my memories.

Preparation time: 15 minutes + cooling
Cooking time: 30–35 minutes
Makes 24 large cupcakes

coloured sugar, to decorate

Red velvet cupcakes
380 g (13¼ oz) plain flour
30 g (1 oz) cocoa powder
1 teaspoon salt
2 dessertspoons powdered red food colouring
300 ml (10½ oz) grapeseed oil
275 g (9¾ oz) caster sugar
2 large eggs
1 teaspoon grenadine syrup
1 teaspoon vanilla extract
200 ml (7 fl oz) buttermilk
1¼ teaspoons baking soda
1½ teaspoons white vinegar

Cream cheese frosting
(see recipe on page 10)

Preheat the oven to 170°C (fan oven 150°C), Gas Mark 3½.

Mix the flour, cocoa powder, salt and food colouring in a bowl. Put the oil and sugar in the bowl of an electric mixer with a paddle attachment and mix at a medium speed until combined. Beat in the eggs, one at a time, scraping down the sides as you go. With the mixer at a very low speed, slowly add the syrup, then the vanilla extract. Add the flour in two batches, alternating with the buttermilk and being careful not to overwork the batter.

Mix the baking soda and vinegar together and add to the batter. Beat for 20 seconds.

Spoon the batter into cupcake moulds lined with paper cases until they are two-thirds full. Bake for 30–35 minutes until a skewer inserted into a cake comes out clean. Leave to cool completely.

Make the cream cheese frosting following the method on page 10 and decorate the cupcakes. Sprinkle a pinch of coloured sugar on each. Leave in the fridge for at least 2 hours to set the icing.

These cupcakes are best if made a day ahead of applying the frosting. Store, decorated or plain, in an airtight container for up to 2 days or in the refrigerator for a week, or freeze unfrosted for up to 2 months.

Variations: For black velvet cupcakes, replace the red food colouring with 2 teaspoons of black food colouring and the grenadine syrup with 2 teaspoons of liquorice syrup and 1 dessertspoon of extra caster sugar. For blue velvet cupcakes, use 2 teaspoons of blue food colouring, 2 teaspoons of violet syrup and 1 dessertspoon of extra caster sugar.

Chocolate curry cupcakes with coconut and lemongrass buttercream

Devil's food cake is another American classic. It has a lighter texture than the basic chocolate cupcake and a deep chocolate taste. Here, it gets an Indo-Asian twist.

Preparation time: 30 minutes + cooling
Cooking time: 20–25 minutes
Makes 30 large cupcakes

100 g (3½ oz) large, dried coconut flakes, to decorate

Chocolate curry cupcakes
95 g (3¼ oz) cocoa powder
350 ml (12¼ fl oz) boiling water
4 large eggs
2 teaspoons chocolate extract (optional)
420 g (14¾ oz) plain flour
450 g (15¾ oz) caster sugar
2½ teaspoons curry powder
1 teaspoon baking soda
1 teaspoon salt
290 g (10¼ oz) unsalted butter

Coconut and lemongrass buttercream
10 cm (4 inch) lemongrass stalk, finely grated
120 ml (4¼ fl oz) coconut milk
200 g (7 oz) unsalted butter, at room temperature
800 g (1 lb 11 oz) icing sugar

Preheat the oven to 170°C (fan oven 150°C), Gas Mark 3½.

Mix the cocoa powder and boiling water together until smooth. Mix together the eggs, a quarter of the cocoa mixture and the chocolate extract, if using.

In a large mixing bowl combine the remaining dry ingredients. Using an electric mixer, add the butter and the remaining cocoa mixture and beat slowly, until all the dry ingredients are moist. Increase the speed to medium and beat for 1–2 minutes. Scrape down the sides then add the egg mixture in two batches, beating for 30 seconds after each addition.

Spoon the batter into cupcake moulds lined with paper cases until they are two-thirds full. The cupcakes will rise while baking and fall back a bit while cooling. Bake for 20–25 minutes until a skewer inserted into a cake comes out clean. Leave to cool completely.

Add the grated lemongrass to the coconut milk and set aside. Put the butter and half the sugar in a large mixing bowl, mix for 30 seconds using an electric mixer, then add the coconut milk and lemongrass. Mix on a medium speed until smooth and creamy, about 4 minutes.

Gradually add the rest of the sugar, one cup at a time, beating very well after each addition. Continue to beat until the buttercream has reached a thickness to spread well.

Use immediately or store in an airtight container at room temperature for up to 3 days.

Using a spoon, put 1–2 tablespoons of frosting on each cupcake. Decorate with the coconut flakes before the frosting sets.

Green tea cupcakes with white chocolate cream cheese frosting

What a delicate little cupcake!

Preparation time: 25 minutes + cooling
Cooking time: 25–30 minutes
Makes 12 large cupcakes

60 g (2 oz) powdered green tea, to decorate

Green tea cupcakes
60 ml (2 oz) milk
4 large egg whites
1 teaspoon vanilla extract
225 g (8 oz) plain flour
200 g (7 oz) caster sugar
1 teaspoon baking powder
½ teaspoon salt
1½ dessertspoons powdered green tea
190 g (6¾ oz) unsalted butter

White chocolate cream cheese frosting
225 g (8 oz) white chocolate, broken into pieces
450 g (1 lb) cream cheese, at room temperature
85 g (3 oz) unsalted butter, at room temperature
1 teaspoon vanilla extract

Preheat the oven to 170°C (fan oven 150°C), Gas Mark 3½.

Mix the milk, egg whites and vanilla extract together and set aside.

Mix the dry ingredients together. Add the butter and half the egg mixture. Beat slowly using an electric mixer until all the dry ingredients are moist. Increase the speed of the mixer and beat for 1 minute.

Scrape down the sides and add the rest of the egg mixture in two halves, beating for 30 seconds between each addition. Scrape down the sides again and beat for a further 10 seconds. Fill paper cases lining cupcake moulds three-quarters full. This batter will rise less than the others.

Bake for 25–30 minutes until a skewer inserted into a cake comes out clean. Leave to cool completely.

For the frosting, melt the white chocolate in a bowl over a pan of simmering water until smooth. Remove from the heat and allow to cool for about 10 minutes. Beat the cream cheese, butter and vanilla together until smooth. Add the melted chocolate and beat well for 1–3 minutes. Use immediately, or keep covered at room temperature for up to 3 hours. The frosting will set when placed in the refrigerator.

Pipe the frosting on to the cupcakes with a ribbon nozzle, then sprinkle with the green tea. Store the frosted cupcakes in an airtight container for up to 2 days or in the refrigerator for a week.

Spiced pumpkin cupcakes with maple syrup cream cheese frosting

Preparation time: 30 minutes + cooling + 30–40 minutes chilling
Cooking time: 20–25 minutes
Makes 24 large cupcakes

Pumpkin cupcakes

300 g (10½ oz) chopped pumpkin flesh
100 g (3½ oz) unsalted butter
220 g (7¾ oz) brown sugar
70 g (2½ oz) caster sugar
315 g (11 oz) plain flour
2 teaspoons baking powder
1 teaspoon bicarbonate of soda
1 teaspoon cinnamon
1 teaspoon ground ginger
½ teaspoon grated nutmeg
⅛ teaspoon ground cloves
½ teaspoon salt
1 teaspoon freshly ground black pepper
2 large eggs
120 ml (4¼ fl oz) buttermilk

Maple syrup cream cheese frosting

450 g (1 lb) cream cheese, at room temperature
115 g (4 oz) unsalted butter, at room temperature
300 g (10½ oz) icing sugar
80 g (2¾ oz) maple syrup, plus extra to serve (optional)

Preheat the oven to 170°C (fan oven 150°C), Gas Mark 3½.

Prepare the pumpkin purée: boil the pumpkin until soft then purée with a mixer or fork. Place the mashed pumpkin in a sieve to drain the excess water. Alternatively, you could use canned pumpkin with no additives.

Using an electric mixer with a paddle attachment, beat the butter and both sugars on a medium speed for about 3 minutes until fluffy. Sift the remaining dry ingredients into a bowl. Add the eggs to the mixer, one at a time, scraping down the sides after each addition. Add the flour mixture in two batches, alternating with the buttermilk and beginning and ending with the flour. Beat in the pumpkin until smooth.

Spoon the batter into cupcake moulds lined with paper cases, filling the cases up to halfway. These work very well small and large. Bake for 20–25 minutes until a skewer inserted into a cake comes out clean. Leave to cool completely before frosting.

Using an electric mixer, beat the cream cheese and butter on a medium speed until smooth. Slowly add the sugar and beat until light and fluffy. Add the maple syrup and beat for about 5–7 minutes or until smooth. Refrigerate for 30–40 minutes before using. The frosting can be kept in the refrigerator for up to 6 days.

Apply the frosting with a spoon or spatula and drizzle with a little extra maple syrup if desired.

You can store the frosted cupcakes in the refrigerator for up to 5 days.

Pistachio cupcakes

Since this is a deconstructed then constructed cupcake, paper cases aren't needed. Bake the cupcakes in silicone moulds without cases, or use a traditional cupcake mould with paper cases and remove the cases after the cupcakes have cooled.

Preparation time: 40 minutes + cooling
Cooking time: 40–50 minutes
Makes 12–16 large cupcakes

Pistachio cupcakes
115 g (4 oz) shelled pistachios
50 g (1¾ oz) ground almonds
190 g (6¾ oz) unsalted butter
250 g (8¾ oz) caster sugar
4 large eggs
½ teaspoon vanilla extract
2 teaspoons pistachio extract
4–6 drops green food colouring
75 g (2½ oz) plain flour

Fondant icing
juice of 1–2 lemons
240 g (8½ oz) icing sugar

Vanilla buttercream
(see recipe on page 10)

Preheat the oven to 150°C (fan oven 130°C), Gas Mark 2.

Toast the pistachios in the oven for 10 minutes, let them cool, then finely grind. Mix with the ground almonds and set aside.

Using an electric mixer with a paddle attachment, beat the butter and sugar until light and fluffy. Beat in the eggs one at a time, add the vanilla and pistachio extracts and food colouring and mix well. Gently mix in the nut mixture then sift in the flour. Mix, scraping down the sides.

Spoon the batter into cupcake moulds so they are two-thirds full. Bake for 40–50 minutes until a skewer inserted into a cake comes out clean. Leave to cool completely before cutting and assembling.

Make the fondant icing: with a fork, add 1 teaspoon of lemon juice to the icing sugar and mix well. Continue to add the lemon juice in small amounts until the icing consistency is thick but still drips off the fork.

Make the vanilla buttercream, following the method on page 10.

Cut the cooled pistachio cupcakes in half (removing any paper cases if used) and turn upside down. Place 1½ tablespoons of vanilla buttercream on the bottom half, replace the top half, then drizzle with the fondant icing. The icing will become firm after about 4 minutes.

Apricot cupcakes with ginger buttercream

Preparation time: 30 minutes +
  cooling
Cooking time: 25–30 minutes
Makes 12 large cupcakes

6 pieces candied ginger, cut in half

Apricot cupcakes
(see pound cake cupcakes recipe
  on page 8)
330 g (11½ oz) fresh apricots, each
  cut into eight pieces

Ginger buttercream
200 g (7 oz) unsalted butter, at
  room temperature
800 g (1 lb 12 oz) icing sugar
120 ml (4¼ fl oz) double cream
1 teaspoon ground ginger
1½ teaspoons fresh ginger, grated

Make the apricot cupcakes following the pound cake cupcake method on page 8, adding the apricots to the mixture. Fill the cupcake moulds three-quarters full for a beautiful, high cupcake. Leave to cool completely before decorating.

To make the buttercream, put the butter and half the sugar in a large mixing bowl. Using an electric mixer, mix for 30 seconds, then add the cream and both gingers. Mix on a medium speed for about 4 minutes until smooth and creamy. Gradually add the rest of the sugar, little by little, beating very well after each addition. Continue to beat until the buttercream has reached a thickness to spread well.

Use immediately or store in an airtight container at room temperature for up to 3 days. The buttercream will set when placed in the refrigerator.

Use a spoon or spatula to apply the frosting to the cupcakes. Top each with half a piece of candied ginger.

Coffee cupcakes with café au lait buttercream and white chocolate

Perfect for pulling an all-nighter!

Preparation time: 20 minutes + cooling
Cooking time: 20–25 minutes
Makes 16 large cupcakes

100 g (3½ oz) white chocolate, to decorate

Coffee cupcakes
115 g (4 oz) dark chocolate (70% cocoa solids), broken into pieces
400 g (14 oz) caster sugar
220 g (7¾ oz) plain flour
¾ teaspoon bicarbonate of soda
½ teaspoon salt
225 ml (8 fl oz) hot coffee
115 g (4 oz) crème fraîche
120 ml (4¼ fl oz) grapeseed oil
2 large eggs

Café au lait buttercream
2 teaspoons instant coffee
120 ml (4¼ fl oz) double cream
1 teaspoon coffee extract
200 g (7 oz) unsalted butter, at room temperature
800 g (1 lb 12 oz) icing sugar

Preheat the oven to 170°C (fan oven 150°C), Gas Mark 3½.

Melt the chocolate in a bowl over a pan of simmering water. Remove from the heat and set aside.

Sift the sugar, flour, bicarbonate of soda and salt together in a large bowl. Using an electric mixer with a paddle attachment, mix the coffee, crème fraîche and oil together. Add the eggs one at a time, scraping down the sides and mixing well. Gradually add the chocolate and mix until combined. Slowly add the dry ingredients and mix until well blended. Scrape down the sides.

Two-thirds fill cupcake moulds lined with paper cases. Bake for 20–25 minutes until a skewer inserted into a cake comes out clean. Leave to cool completely before frosting.

To make the buttercream, dissolve the instant coffee in the cream, add the coffee extract, mix and set aside. Put the butter and half the sugar in a bowl, beat for 30 seconds, then add the cream mixture. Using an electric mixer, mix on a medium speed for about 4 minutes, until smooth and creamy. Gradually add the rest of the sugar, one cup at a time, beating very well after each addition. Continue to beat until the buttercream has reached a thickness to spread well.

Use immediately or store in an airtight container at room temperature for up to 3 days. The buttercream will set when placed in the refrigerator.

Use a piping bag with a 6-point star nozzle to apply the buttercream. Shave the white chocolate with a grater or vegetable peeler. Sprinkle the shavings on the frosted cupcakes before the buttercream sets.

Crêpes Suzette cupcakes

So what's American about this? Hmm....probably nothing. But how can you resist the wonderful flavours of crêpes Suzette? And now these flavours are available to you in a rich, intense cupcake. (Adapted from a recipe by Trish Deseine – Thanks!)

Preparation time: 30 minutes + cooling
Cooking time: 30–35 minutes
Makes 16 large cupcakes

Cupcakes
435 g (15¼ oz) plain flour
1 tablespoon baking powder
1 teaspoon bicarbonate of soda
½ teaspoon salt
190 g (6¾ oz) salted butter
400 g (14 oz) caster sugar
4 large eggs
295 ml (10 fl oz) buttermilk
zest of 1 large orange
18 teaspoons Grand Marnier

Suzette syrup
2 oranges
200 g (7 oz) salted butter
200 g (7 oz) caster sugar
300 ml (10½ fl oz) Grand Marnier

Preheat the oven to 170°C (fan oven 150°C), Gas Mark 3½.

Sift the flour, baking powder, bicarbonate of soda and salt together.

Using an electric mixer with a paddle attachment, beat the butter until soft. Slowly add the sugar and beat for about 3 minutes until light and fluffy. Add the eggs one at a time, beating for 20 seconds after each addition. Scrape down the sides. Mix the buttermilk with the orange zest and 2 teaspoons of Grand Marnier.

Add the dry ingredients to the butter mixture in three stages, alternating with the buttermilk mixture and beginning and ending with the flour mixture. Be careful not to overwork the batter.

Two-thirds fill cupcake moulds. Bake for 30–35 minutes until a skewer inserted into a cake comes out clean.

While the cupcakes are still in their moulds, spoon 1 teaspoon of Grand Marnier on each cake. Leave to cool completely before turning out.

Cut the orange rind into 16 pieces about 4 x 8 mm (¼ x ½ inch) long. Juice the oranges and set aside. Melt the butter in a large saucepan, add the sugar, Grand Marnier, orange juice and rind. Bring to a boil, stirring continuously, then reduce the heat to medium, stirring occasionally until the sauce thickens and begins to stick to the spoon. Remove from the heat immediately. The syrup will continue to thicken as it cools. Use at once.

Place the cupcakes upside down on a wire rack and spoon the syrup over the cakes, making sure a piece of rind is on top of each. Store in an airtight container for up to 2 days.

Tip: Bake in silicone moulds without paper cases, or use traditional moulds with paper cases and remove the cases after the cupcakes have cooled.

Chocolate chilli cupcakes topped with chocolate ganache

When I am feeling nostalgic and fancy Mexican food, the Dulce de leche cupcakes (see page 56) and this combination of chilli and chocolate helps it all feel better. These are best made as mini cupcakes. They are based on the Chocolate-chocolate cupcakes (page 14), with a few alterations.

Preparation time: 35 minutes + cooling
Cooking time: 12–20 minutes
Makes 36–40 little cupcakes

2 tablespoons chilli flakes, to decorate

Chocolate chilli cupcakes
75 g (2½ oz) cocoa powder
230 ml (8 fl oz) boiling water
3 large eggs
1 teaspoon chocolate extract (optional)
280 g (10 oz) plain flour
300 g (10½ oz) caster sugar
1 tablespoon baking powder
¾ teaspoon salt
1–2 teaspoons chilli powder
190 g (6¾ oz) unsalted butter

Chocolate ganache
385 ml (13½ fl oz) double cream
340 g (12 oz) dark chocolate, broken into pieces
40 g (1½ oz) unsalted butter, at room temperature

Preheat the oven to 160°C (fan oven 140°C), Gas Mark 3.

Mix the cocoa powder and boiling water together until smooth. Mix together the eggs, a quarter of the cocoa mixture and the chocolate extract, if using.

Using an electric mixer, combine the remaining dry ingredients in a large bowl and slowly mix. Add the butter and remaining cocoa mixture and beat slowly, until all the dry ingredients are moist. Increase the speed to medium and beat for 1–2 minutes. Scrape down the sides then add the egg mixture in two batches, beating for 30 seconds after each addition and scraping down the sides.

Two-thirds fill cupcake moulds lined with paper cases. The cupcakes will rise while baking and fall back a bit while cooling. Bake for 12–20 minutes until a skewer inserted into a cake comes out clean. Leave to cool completely.

To make the ganache, heat the cream and remove from the heat when it is just below boiling point. Add the chocolate and mix gently without stopping until you have a smooth paste. Add the softened butter and mix well. Leave to cool for around 10 minutes before using.

Gently spoon a small amount of partially cooled ganache on to each cupcake. Sprinkle with chilli flakes. Do not refrigerate. Store in an airtight container for up to 4 days.

Lemon meringue pie cupcakes

This assembled cupcake reminds me of one of my favourite pies. Use shop bought lemon curd and make the meringue tops ahead. They can be stored in an airtight container for a few days. Assemble the cupcakes just before serving.

Preparation time: 50 minutes + cooling
Cooking time: 30–40 minutes for the meringues, 25–30 minutes for the cupcakes
Makes 12 cupcakes

250 g (8¾ oz) lemon curd

Meringue tops
6 egg whites, at room temperature
½ teaspoon cream of tartar
½ teaspoon cornflour
100 g (3½ oz) caster sugar

Lemon cupcakes
120 g (4¼ oz) plain flour
¼ teaspoon bicarbonate of soda
¼ teaspoon salt
165 g (5¾ oz) caster sugar, plus
  1 tablespoon
3 large eggs, separated
60 ml (2 fl oz) grapeseed oil
80 ml (2¾ fl oz) water
1 tablespoon lemon juice
2 tablespoons lemon zest
  (about 3 lemons)
¼ teaspoon cream of tartar

Preheat the oven to 100°C (fan oven 80°C), Gas Mark ¼.

Using an electic mixer with a whisk attachment, beat the egg whites until foamy. Add the cream of tartar and cornflour. Beat until soft peaks form. Add the sugar a little at a time, beating well after each addition. Beat until the peaks are glossy.

Spoon the mixture on to a baking sheet lined with baking parchment, forming rounds 6 cm (2½ inches) in diameter and 3 cm (1¼ inches) high. Create fancy peaks using the back of a spoon. Bake for 30–40 minutes until the peaks turn golden and the meringues are slightly firm to the touch. Cool and store or use immediately.

For the cupcakes, preheat the oven to 160°C (fan oven 140°C), Gas Mark 3. Sift the flour, bicarbonate of soda, salt and sugar together and set aside.

In a large bowl, whisk the egg yolks, oil, water, lemon juice and lemon zest until well combined. Add the sifted dry ingredients and beat well. Using an electric mixer with a whisk attachment, whisk the egg whites until foamy. Add the cream of tartar and whisk on high until soft peaks form. Slowly add the 1 tablespoon of sugar and beat on high for about 1 minute.

Fold the egg whites into the other mixture but do not overwork. Spoon the batter into 12 large cupcake moulds lined with paper cases. Bake for 25–30 minutes until the cupcakes are golden in colour and a skewer inserted into a cake comes out clean. Leave to cool completely.

To assemble, put about 1 tablespoon of lemon curd on each cupcake then top with a meringue hat.

Sesame cupcakes with tahini buttercream

Preparation time: 35 minutes +
cooling
Cooking time: 30–35 minutes
Makes 24 large cupcakes

2 tablespoons black sesame seeds,
to decorate

Sesame cupcakes
(see recipe on page 12)
2 tablespoons white sesame seeds

Tahini buttercream
200 g (7 oz) unsalted butter,
at room temperature
800 g (1 lb 12 oz) icing sugar
3 tablespoons double cream
3 tablespoons tahini

Make the cupcakes following the method on page 12, adding the sesame seeds to the dry ingredients. You will only need ½ a teaspoon of vanilla extract. Leave to cool completely.

For the buttercream, put the butter and half the sugar in a large mixing bowl. Using an electric mixer, mix for 30 seconds, then add the cream and tahini. Mix on a medium speed for about 4 minutes until smooth and creamy. Gradually add the rest of the sugar, one cup at a time, beating very well after each addition. Continue to beat until the buttercream has reached a thickness to spread well. Use immediately or store in an airtight container at room temperature for up to 3 days. The buttercream will set when placed in the refrigerator.

Pipe the tahini buttercream on to the cakes with a ribbon piping nozzle, then sprinkle with black sesame seeds.

Store decorated or plain in an airtight container for up to 2 days or in the refrigerator for a week.

严禁推销
商贩入内

LOS AN
1955—
BIRTH
ARTIST

8 March —

Los Angeles has
diverse artistic so
marked by a con
aesthetic movem
Its art is nourish
"city-wor

Dulce de leche cupcakes

Inspired by the classic Mexican three milk cake. A strong cup of coffee is a great accompaniment.

Preparation time: 30 minutes + cooling
Cooking time: 30–35 minutes
Makes 24 large cupcakes

160 ml (5½ fl oz) double cream
300 g (10½ oz) dulce de leche

Cupcakes
435 g (15¼ oz) plain flour
1 tablespoon baking powder
1 teaspoon bicarbonate of soda
2 teaspoons cinnamon
½ teaspoon salt
190 g (6¾ oz) salted butter
400 g (14 oz) caster sugar
4 large eggs
260 ml (9 fl oz) buttermilk
1 teaspoon vanilla extract

Vanilla buttercream
(see recipe on page 10)

Preheat the oven to 170°C (fan oven 150°C), Gas Mark 3½.

Sift the flour, baking powder, bicarbonate of soda, cinnamon and salt together and set aside.

Using an electric mixer with a paddle attachment, beat the butter until soft. Slowly add the sugar and beat for about 3 minutes until light and fluffy. Add the eggs one at a time, beating for 20 seconds after each addition and scraping down the sides.

In a small bowl, mix the buttermilk with the vanilla extract. Add the sifted dry ingredients to the butter mixture in three stages, alternating with the buttermilk mixture and beginning and ending with the flour. Be careful not to overmix.

Spoon the batter into cupcake moulds lined with paper cases until they are two-thirds full. Bake for 30–35 minutes until a skewer inserted into a cake comes out clean.

While still warm, brush the cupcakes with the cream and allow to cool for at least an hour (you could also make them the day before).

Make the vanilla buttercream following the method on page 10.

Once the cupcakes are fully cooled, spoon 1 teaspoon of dulce de leche on top of each cupcake, pipe on the vanilla buttercream and finish with a further drizzle of dulce de leche.

The cakes can be stored decorated or plain in an airtight container for up to 2 days or in the refrigerator for a week.

Cherry rhubarb cupcakes

The combination of cherries with rhubarb was my father's favourite. The great colour in the vanilla buttercream is made using a mix of green and yellow food colouring.

Preparation time: 30 minutes +
cooling
Cooking time: 20–30 minutes
Makes 12 large cupcakes

Cherry rhubarb cupcakes
225 g (8 oz) cherries, fresh or frozen
225 g (8 oz) rhubarb, fresh or frozen
3 tablespoons icing sugar
300 g (10½ oz) plain flour
150 g (5¼ oz) caster sugar
1½ tablespoons baking powder
½ teaspoon bicarbonate of soda
¼ teaspoon salt
85 g (3 oz) cream cheese
1 teaspoon lemon juice
½ teaspoon vanilla extract
2 large eggs
50 g (1¾ oz) unsalted butter,
softened
120 ml (4¼ fl oz) milk

Vanilla buttercream
(see recipe on page 10)
yellow food colouring
green food colouring

Preheat the oven to 170°C (fan oven 150°C), Gas Mark 3½.

Frozen fruit is best for cupcakes, but fresh also works. If using frozen cherries, remove them from the freezer when you begin to assemble all the other ingredients. They don't need to thaw fully. If using fresh cherries, clean them and remove the stones. For frozen rhubarb, thaw, mix with the icing sugar and set aside. For fresh rhubarb, clean and cut into 2 cm (¾ inch) pieces. Place in a pan with a small amount of water and cook for 5 minutes. Remove from the heat, cool to room temperature, stir in the icing sugar and set aside.

Sift the flour, caster sugar, baking powder, bicarbonate of soda and salt together and set aside.

Using an electric mixer with a paddle attachment, mix the cream cheese, lemon juice and vanilla extract until smooth.

Add the eggs and mix well. Scrape down the sides, add the softened butter and mix for 20 seconds. Add the milk and mix until well combined. Slowly add the dry ingredients, mixing until well combined. Be careful not to overmix.

Line cupcake moulds with paper cases and drop 2–3 cherries and 2–3 pieces of rhubarb into each case. Fill the cases two-thirds full with mixture then add the remaining fruit, divided between each cupcake. Bake for 20–30 minutes until a skewer inserted into a cake comes out clean. Leave to cool completely.

Make the vanilla buttercream following the method on page 10, adding a few drops of food colouring until you have achieved the colour you want. Spread on to the cupcakes.

Store, decorated or plain, in an airtight container for up to 2 days or in the refrigerator for a week.

Cardamom cupcakes with chocolate swirl meringue frosting

Swirling the chocolate into the Italian meringue is impressive, yummy and easy to do!

Preparation time: 35 minutes + cooling
Cooking time: 30–35 minutes
Makes 24 large cupcakes

Cardamom cupcakes
(see recipe on page 12)
2 teaspoons cinnamon
2 teaspoons ground cardamom
½ teaspoon vanilla extract

Chocolate meringue frosting
100 g (3½ oz) dark chocolate, broken into pieces
300 g (10½ oz) Italian meringue (see recipe on page 10)

Make the cupcakes following the method on page 12, adding the cinnamon and cardamom to the dry ingredients. You will only need ½ a teaspoon of vanilla extract. Leave to cool completely.

For the frosting, melt the chocolate in a bowl over a pan of simmering water. Set aside while making the Italian meringue following the method on page 10.

Fit a piping bag with a large round nozzle. With a pastry brush, brush the melted chocolate inside the piping bag in three stripes. Fill the piping bag with the meringue mixture and generously pipe on to the cupcakes. Wow!

Dark chocolate cupcakes with orange cream filling and burnt orange buttercream

Preparation time: 40 minutes + cooling
Cooking time: 20–25 minutes
Makes 24 large cupcakes

Dark chocolate cupcakes
(see recipe on page 14)

Orange cream filling
200 ml (7 fl oz) double cream
250 g (8¾ oz) mascarpone
finely grated zest of 1 large orange
a little orange food colouring

Burnt orange buttercream
200 g (7 oz) unsalted butter, at room temperature, plus
1 tablespoon
grated zest of 2 large oranges
juice of 1 large orange
3 tablespoons caster sugar
800 g (1 lb 12 oz) icing sugar
60 ml (2 fl oz) double cream
a little orange food colouring

Make the cupcakes following the method on page 14 and leave to cool completely. Since they will be filled, do not fill the moulds more than halfway.

For the orange cream filling, whip the cream until it thickens and forms peaks. Add the mascarpone and beat for 3 minutes then add the orange zest and food colouring and mix. If necessary, keep in the fridge for 2 hours.

For the burnt orange buttercream, melt the 1 tablespoon of butter in a pan, add the orange zest, orange juice and caster sugar. Cook slowly until the mixture begins to turn a golden colour. Remove from the heat and set aside.

Put the butter and half the icing sugar in a large mixing bowl. Using an electric mixer, mix for 30 seconds, then add the cream and the orange mixture. Mix on medium for about 4 minutes until smooth and creamy. Gradually add the rest of the sugar, beating very well after each addition. At this point add the food colouring, a tiny bit at a time to achieve a slightly darker colour than used in the cream filling. Continue to beat until the buttercream has reached a thickness to spread well. Use immediately or store in an airtight container at room temperature for up to 3 days.

When the cupcakes are completely cool, cut off the top in an inverted pyramid shape. Slice the pyramid off the 'lid' so that the lid is flat, then gently carve out a hole in the cupcake. Fill the hole with the cream filling and replace the lid. Using a medium, round nozzle, pipe on the burnt orange buttercream. Refrigerate for a minimum of 2 hours and remove from the refrigerator 20 minutes before serving.

My 'hostess' cupcakes

This type of dessert can be found in the US in little packages of two. The first time I saw them made with more gourmet ingredients was when my friend Mercy brought them to a party. They received nostalgic smiles before eating and comments of "oh, my!" after each bite.

Preparation time: 40 minutes + cooling
Cooking time: 20–25 minutes
Makes 36 large cupcakes

Dark chocolate cupcakes
95 g (3½ oz) cocoa powder
350 ml (12¼ fl oz) boiling water
4 large eggs
½ teaspoon vanilla extract
2 teaspoons chocolate extract (optional)
280 g (10 oz) plain flour
300 g (10½ oz) caster sugar
1 tablespoon baking powder
1 teaspoon salt
290 g (10¼ oz) unsalted butter

Cream filling
200 ml (7 fl oz) double cream
250 g (8¾ oz) mascarpone

Dark chocolate ganache
(see recipe on page 24)

Fondant icing
(see recipe on page 42)

Preheat the oven to 170°C (fan oven 150°C), Gas Mark 3½.

Mix the cocoa powder and boiling water together until smooth. Mix the eggs, a quarter of the cocoa mixture and the vanilla and chocolate extracts together in a medium bowl

In a large mixing bowl, combine the remaining dry ingredients and slowly mix with a whisk. Using an electric mixer, add the butter and remaining cocoa mixture and beat slowly until all the dry ingredients are moist. Increase the speed to medium and beat for 1–2 minutes. Scrape down the sides then add the egg mixture in two batches, beating for 30 seconds after each addition.

Spoon the batter into cupcake moulds lined with paper cases until they are three-quarters full. Bake for 20–25 minutes until a skewer inserted into a cake comes out clean. Leave to cool. They are best if made a day ahead.

For the cream filling, using an electric mixer whisk the cream on high for 5–8 minutes until thick and forming peaks. Add the mascarpone and beat for 3 minutes. This can be made and stored in the refrigerator for 2 hours.

Make the dark chocolate ganache and the fondant icing following the methods on pages 24 and 42.

When the cupcakes are completely cool, cut off the top in an inverted pyramid shape. Slice the pyramid off the 'lid' so that the lid is flat, then gently carve out a hole in the cupcake. Fill the hole with the cream filling and replace the 'lid'. Gently spoon the ganache on to the cupcakes, using the paper cases as a guide. Do not let the ganache overflow the cases. Cool well (but do not refrigerate) before piping on the fondant icing using a very small round nozzle. These cupcakes will not keep in the fridge.

Fondant icing

You can buy rolled fondant icing or make your own. It can be coloured and shaped like modelling clay.

Preparation time: 20–30 minutes
Makes 1 kg (2 lb 4 oz) fondant icing

900 g (2 lb) icing sugar, sifted
50 ml (1¾ fl oz) cold water
1 tablespoon powdered gelatine
50 ml (1¾ fl oz) glucose
1½ tablespoons glycerine
food colouring (optional)

Sift the sugar into a large bowl (do not use metal) and make a well in the centre.

Pour the water into a small saucepan and sprinkle the gelatine on top to soften for about 5 minutes. Begin to heat the gelatine and stir until it is dissolved and clear. Do not boil. Turn off the heat and add the glucose and glycerine, stirring until well blended. Pour into the well of sugar and mix until all of the sugar is blended. Use your hands to knead the icing until it becomes stiff. Add small amounts of icing sugar if the mixture is too sticky.

Form the mixture into a ball and wrap tightly in cling film. Place in an airtight container. This icing works best if allowed to rest at room temperature for about 8 hours before using, particularly if the weather is humid. Do not refrigerate.

Add a drop of liquid food colouring to the base and knead with your fingers to achieve the desired colours. Flatten with a rolling pin for a smooth covering or to make a flat disk, then cut out your shapes. Roll into balls and other three-dimensional shapes. Use cookie cutters and your imagination! Pieces of fondant icing will stick together when dampened with warm water and a small brush. It will harden when left to dry.

Decorating hints and tips

Dust your hands with cornflour when smoothing fondant icing. This icing keeps a cake fresh for 2 days at room temperature. Do not refrigerate a cake covered with fondant icing.

Rolled icing is versatile. It can be tinted, flavoured, modelled, formed, twisted, imprinted and shaped into numerous decorative pieces.

Before applying fondant icing, a 'sticky' surface should be applied to the cake to help the icing adhere to it. A thin layer of buttercream spread over the cake will help the icing stick.

Fondant icing dries quickly so, while working with it, always keep extra pieces well-wrapped in cling film, as well as the parts on the cake you are not working on.

Once wrapped, unrolled fondant icing keeps for 1–2 months at room temperature. Do not refrigerate or freeze. If it gets too hard, put it in the microwave for a few seconds to soften – it will be easier to knead.

If tiny cracks appear in the surface of the icing, knead it a little – the warmth from the kneading or pressure from the rolling pin will make it smooth and satiny. Do not use water to smooth out cracks – water dissolves fondant icing as it is mostly sugar. Instead, use a bit of margarine on your fingertips to repair small tears.

Wedding cupcakes

White on white, with silver and gold accents. Small to large.

Macadamia cupcakes with white chocolate cream cheese frosting

Preparation time: 20 minutes
Cooking time: 25–30 minutes
Makes 12 large cupcakes

silver and gold dragées or glitter, to decorate

Macadamia cupcakes
(see pound cake cupcakes recipe on page 8)
1 teaspoon grated nutmeg
165 g (5¾ oz) macadamia nuts, whole or halved

White chocolate cream cheese frosting
(see recipe on page 38)

Make the cupcakes following the pound cake cupcake method on page 8, adding the nuts to the mixture. Use different sizes of mould and types of paper cases.

Make the frosting following the method on page 38. You can keep the frosting in a covered container for 3 hours at room temperature.

Pipe the frosting on to the cupcakes using a variety of nozzles. Sprinkle with silver and gold dragees or glitter. You can keep the frosted cupcakes in an airtight container for up to 2 days or in the refrigerator for a week.

Snow cupcakes with vanilla mint buttercream

Preparation time: 20 minutes
Cooking time: 25–30 minutes
Makes 12 large cupcakes

Snow cupcakes
(see light vanilla cupcakes recipe on page 8)
3 teaspoons fresh mint leaves, finely chopped

Vanilla mint buttercream
(see recipe on page 10)
2 dessertspoons fresh mint leaves, finely chopped

Make the cupcakes following the light vanilla cupcakes method on page 8, replacing the cardamom with the mint leaves. Use moulds of varied sizes and different types of paper cases.

Make the vanilla buttercream following the method on page 10 and adding the mint leaves with the sugar.

Frost the cakes with the vanilla buttercream.

Index

Conversion tables

The tables below are only approximate and are meant to be used as a guide only.

Approximate American/ European conversions

	USA	Metric	Imperial
brown sugar	1 cup	170 g	6 oz
butter	1 stick	115 g	4 oz
butter/ margarine/ lard	1 cup	225 g	8 oz
caster and granulated sugar	2 level tablespoons	30 g	1 oz
caster and granulated sugar	1 cup	225 g	8 oz
currants	1 cup	140 g	5 oz
flour	1 cup	140 g	5 oz
golden syrup	1 cup	350 g	12 oz
ground almonds	1 cup	115 g	4 oz
sultanas/ raisins	1 cup	200 g	7 oz

Approximate American/ European conversions

American	European
1 teaspoon	1 teaspoon/ 5 ml
½ fl oz	1 tablespoon/ ½ fl oz/ 15 ml
¼ cup	4 tablespoons/ 2 fl oz/ 50 ml
½ cup plus 2 tablespoons	¼ pint/ 5 fl oz/ 150 ml
1¼ cups	½ pint/ 10 fl oz/ 300 ml
1 pint/ 16 fl oz	1 pint/ 20 fl oz/ 600 ml
2½ pints (5 cups)	1.2 litres/ 2 pints
10 pints	4.5 litres/ 8 pints

Liquid measures

Imperial	ml	fl oz
1 teaspoon	5	
2 tablespoons	30	
4 tablespoons	60	
¼ pint/ 1 gill	150	5
⅓ pint	200	7
½ pint	300	10
¾ pint	425	15
1 pint	600	20
1¾ pints	1000 (1 litre)	35

Oven temperatures

American	Celsius	Fahrenheit	Gas Mark
Cool	130	250	½
Very slow	140	275	1
Slow	150	300	2
Moderate	160	320	3
Moderate	180	350	4
Moderately hot	190	375	5
Fairly hot	200	400	6
Hot	220	425	7
Very hot	230	450	8
Extremely hot	240	475	9

Other useful measurements

Measurement	Metric	Imperial
1 American cup	225 ml	8 fl oz
1 egg, size 3	50 ml	2 fl oz
1 egg white	30 ml	1 fl oz
1 rounded tablespoon flour	30 g	1 oz
1 rounded tablespoon cornflour	30 g	1 oz
1 rounded tablespoon caster sugar	30 g	1 oz
2 level teaspoons gelatine	10 g	¼ oz